D[illegible] MADISON

FIRST LADY

by Bette Beer

HOUGHTON MIFFLIN BOSTON

Dolley Madison

Dolley Payne was born
in 1768.
She grew up in Virginia.

James Madison

Later, Dolley met
James Madison.
In 1794 Dolley and
James Madison married.

The White House

In 1809 James Madison became President of the United States. The wife of the President is called the First Lady. Dolley became the First Lady.

The Red Room in the White House

They lived in the White House.
It is in Washington, D.C.
Dolley made the White House beautiful.

Dancing at a party

Dolley wore beautiful clothes.
She had dinner parties.
She made people feel welcome
in her home.

The Federal Room in the White House

Many people visited
the White House.
Dolley always remembered
people's names.
She was a great hostess.

British soldiers at war

In 1814 the United States was at war with Britain. President Madison had to leave Washington, D.C.

A British attack

Now Dolley was in charge of the White House. British soldiers were coming close to Washington, D.C.

Dolley saved important papers.

Dolley knew that she had to leave the White House. She wanted to save some important things.

Dolley saved a painting.

Dolley saved a painting
of President
George Washington.

The White House was burned.

The British soldiers left
Washington, D.C.
The Madisons went back
to the White House.
It had been burned!
They had to live
in another house.

Dolley Madison, First Lady

People thought Dolley
was a hero.
She was very smart.
She was very brave.
Dolley Madison was
an important First Lady.

In 1817 James Madison
finished being President.
Then Dolley and James Madison
left Washington, D.C.

The Madison's house in Virginia

The farm

Dolley and James Madison moved to a farm in Virginia. Dolley welcomed people there.

Dolley Madison was First Lady from 1809 to 1817.
Dolley Madison...

- made the White House beautiful
- had dinner parties
- welcomed people to her home
- was in charge of the White House when the President left
- saved important things
- helped the President in many ways